Susie's Miracle

The Inspiration Behind Susie's Law

by Donna Lawrence

book and cover design by Jennifer Tipton Cappoen

Book and Cover Designer: Jennifer Tipton Cappoen
Copy Editor: Lynn Bemer Coble
Photographers: Erin Arsenault, Jerry Wofford

Published by **Paws and Claws Publishing, LLC**
1589 Skeet Club Road, Suite 102-175
High Point, NC 27265
www.PawsandClawsPublishing.com
info@pawsandclawspublishing.com

ISBN #978-0-9846724-0-0
Printed in the United States
Second Edition

Special Thanks...

I would like to thank my husband Roy, my friend Dana Harbor, and my family and friends for all of their support.

Thank you to everyone behind Susie's Law for all of their hard work and dedication.

A very special thank you to the wonderful people at the Guilford County Animal Shelter, including Director Marsha Williams, for saving Susie.

I also want to thank Roberta and Bob Wall for fostering Susie and for their help in nursing her back to health and in finding her a permanent home.

I would like to thank the man who found Susie in the park and cared enough to call for help.

I would also like to thank Karen Regan with Doggone-it! and Gary Hall and Ally Thomas with Southern Tails for all of the dog training they have provided to Susie and me.

Most of all, I thank God for bringing Susie into my life at a time when I needed her the most.

~Donna Lawrence

This book is dedicated to all of the animals out there that had no voice but that now—thanks to Susie—have been given a voice.

Arise, shine; for thy light is come, and the glory of the Lord is risen upon thee.
Isaiah 60:1

Table of Contents

Table of Contents

Susie

Chapter 1
Alone and in Pain

Sometimes things happen to us that change our lives forever. Sometimes good things come from bad things. I know because I had something horrible happen to me. My name is Susie, and I am a victim of violence and abuse. However, unlike so many animals that suffer in silence at the hands of their owners, I survived. Most people say it was a miracle that a puppy like me survived all that happened.

My new owner says that I survived because of something she calls *mercy*—God's mercy. She says that God's mercy brings hope to all of his creatures big and small. I am one of

 7

the lucky ones, a survivor beyond natural circumstances. With the love and support of my new family and friends, I have become a voice for all of the animals out there needing someone to speak up for them. There is even a new North Carolina law named after me: Susie's Law.

—⚊—

That day started out like any other day. I was ten weeks old and loved to do what any puppy does. I also loved my little boy; he was sweet and smelled good. I had only lived in my home a few weeks, and I did everything I could to let my new family know how much I loved them.

I still don't know what I did to anger the man who had brought me into their home. I only kissed my little boy to show him how much I loved him. I have come to know that the man was irate and in search of someone…*no…something*. Something helpless on which he could take out his anger. I was just a puppy that knew nothing of hate and rage. I knew only the ideas of loyalty and love. But I quickly came to know the effects of uncontrolled anger.

He picked me up so tightly that I could not breathe. Startled, I struggled to get away. I yelped, but I could not get out of his strong, enraged grip. He hit me again and again with his fist and broke my jaw. I was stunned. I began to lose consciousness.

The smell of lighter fluid…its odor was so strong it burned my nose. Then I felt something wet splashing all over me. Finally I heard a sound that I recognized: the lighting of a match. Oh no, everything went dark.

—⁂—

When I regained consciousness, I found myself in a strange place. I was scared and I hurt all over. I started looking for my little boy to see if he was OK. I searched for anything familiar. But with every step I took, I felt intense pain. My back tingled and burned. My ears were bloody and painful. I could hardly open my mouth. I may have been very young, but I knew I needed help immediately. I was so scared. I didn't understand what had happened to me. *Why did this happen? What did I do to make him so angry with me?*

Each day after that I woke up with flies buzzing all around me. I really wanted to scratch the itchy places on my back and head, but it was too painful. Oh how they itched! The hot August sun was beating down on me. I was so thirsty and hungry. After days of this, I had started to get weak, and I wondered if I could go on for another minute. Death was around the corner, and I was beginning to give up.

Nights were worse. I was so cold. And the shadows and

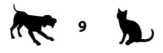

sounds terrified me. I tried to make myself really small and to hide in the bushes so no wild animal would find me. As I went in and out of consciousness, I had nightmares about the bad man standing over me ready to hurt me again. Then I woke up whining and shaking.

—ɰ—

I didn't know how much time had passed. I only knew that even though I felt hopeless, I wanted to live. I was so thirsty that I needed to find water. I began to eat whatever I could find, no matter how badly it hurt to open my mouth and swallow. I frantically searched the ground for food. I ate food from trash cans. I ate sticks, berries, and even dirt. I couldn't find fresh water, so I drank from mud holes. *Where was my little boy? Was anyone looking for me?*

Several days had gone by, and they seemed like an eternity. As time passed, my odds of survival dwindled. My wounds needed care; they had gone untreated for days.

—ɰ—

On August 20, 2009, I awoke again in a weakened, painful state. Oh, how I wished for—no—*needed* someone to give me a helping hand. My mind began to race. My immediate need was food. I stretched and began to hobble along.

 10

I found a tiny mud hole and was sipping all the water I could, when I heard footsteps. I slowly turned my head and caught a glimpse of a human. I had come across other humans in the past few days, but not one had taken notice of me. No one seemed to care.

However, I could tell that this man was different. He had been sent there for one reason: to bring hope to my desperate situation. He got down on one knee and just knelt there. I stared into his shocked, compassionate eyes, and he stared back at me. Then he gently picked me up.

A second chance at life and running with it.

—◦◦◦—

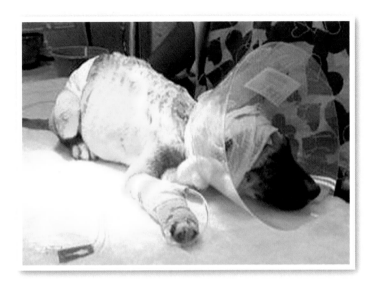

Chapter 2
Shelter

After days of slow agony, my life started moving fast. I had been in the man's arms for only a minute. He immediately got on his cell phone and made a call for help.

While we waited for help to arrive, the man held me and comforted me in ways I had never known. He assured me everything would be all right and said, "Hold on, little gal. You can make it; don't give up now. Help is on its way."

A truck pulled up and I was placed carefully inside a cage in the back. I felt afraid as we drove to an unknown destination. I couldn't help but wonder if I would ever see the kind man again. I began to drift off to sleep and felt my strength drain

 13

out of me. I had nothing left in me.

Suddenly the truck stopped. Its back doors were yanked open, and I was in the arms of another human. As I was being rushed into the Guilford County Animal Shelter, I felt peace come over me. Soft voices shared their concerns. "Poor little baby. What kind of monster would do such a thing?" Immediately, I became their main focus. They knew I was at the point of death.

The caring vet techs took me into a room that was packed with all kinds of medical equipment. It was so bright in there. As they ever so gently placed me upon the table in the center of the room, I listened as they began to discuss what to do next and my chances of survival.

I heard their soft, sympathetic voices. "She has second- and third-degree burns over 60 percent of her body…and look at her ears…they are completely gone! Her jaw is broken and some of her teeth are missing!" I was feeling all of the pains that they were describing.

"We're going to save this little girl. She's a survivor. We all know that it's going to be a long, difficult, painful journey," elaborated the female veterinarian. Hearing those mildly alarming words, I sat up. I knew I had to do something to show her that she was right and I was a survivor. I had come too far

 14

to give up. What could I possibly do to prove to these humans that I was a survivor?

Just then, I had an idea. I knew that if I found her eyes, my eyes would speak the words that my mouth could never say. I turned my head slowly and licked her hand gently. I stared right into her face with my big brown eyes. I was trying to say with my look, "Yes, I am worth saving! I am of value. It may look like my life is over, but it's not. Just give me a chance, and I'll prove to you that I am a survivor."

Then blessed words I had been pleading silently to hear flowed from her lips: "Just look at those loving brown eyes. I could see that this little girl was a fighter. She doesn't want to give up. And we shouldn't give up on our fight for her life."

Within minutes, the atmosphere in the room became charged with energy. Everyone began to work frantically and diligently to ensure my survival.

I had to be bathed and bandaged. My wounds were carefully cleaned. As the doctors and technicians took care of me, their voices spoke soothing words to my soul. How comforting it was to feel the soft, loving hands of humans! Those gentle touches were slowly easing the pain and hurt from my abuse.

 15

Vet Tech Marissa Lea Stadivent

 16

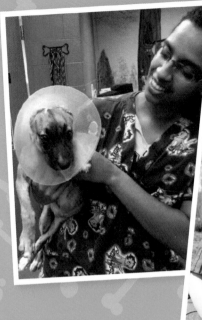

Dr. Ashley Spruill

Guilford County Animal Shelter staff—Second from left: Director Marsha Williams

 17

During my first exam, they found more than 300 fly larvae (wormlike feeding forms hatched from insect eggs) on my back. That discovery helped the humans determine how long I had been abandoned in the park. "Ten days," they said. "She's lucky. These maggots ate away any infection and probably saved her life." I felt lucky, something I had not felt in a couple of weeks.

As my new mom always says to others and to me, *lucky* was not the correct word. God's *mercy* is what saved my life. Looking back on my ordeal, I realized that all of my little blessings were adding up to one thing: purpose. I must have had a purpose on Earth. I would become a symbol of love, hope, and forgiveness to share with the world. I would spread this message to give hope to others.

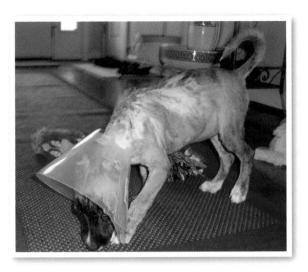

Chapter 3
Susie Went Home with Her Foster Family

As I spent that first night at the animal shelter, some major decisions were being made about my life and recovery. The doctors knew it was going to be a long road ahead. After all, my body was badly burned, and I had gone untreated for almost two weeks. Major portions of my ears were completely gone, and my jaw was broken. My diet for the past ten days had caused severe malnutrition and dehydration.

Everyone involved in my care had a lot of questions. Who would be willing to take me home and care for me? Was there anyone out there who was loving and caring enough to tend to my special needs? Was I adoptable? Would anyone want me

 19

as their pet?

Soon my story got out into the community. The shelter was frantically searching for someone who would be willing to foster me in their home. I had become accustomed to my new caretakers, but at some point, I had to leave.

After extensive evaluations and discussions, the shelter staff had decided that due to my serious injuries, I had to be placed in foster care first. That way, the shelter would continue to treat me and take care of my special needs. They would continue to do what could not be done at home. And they would anesthetize me as needed so my pain during their care would not be unbearable. Later I could be placed with a loving, adoptive family.

I was not ready for a permanent home. The shelter staff had to help me get better so that someone would want to adopt me. Then my adoptive family would not have to worry about the stress or the expense of my ongoing care.

After many calls to shelter supporters, I finally got my big break. A married couple contacted the shelter. They were willing to take me in, care for my every need, and give me the love and attention I so greatly needed. They became my foster parents in September 2009. Their jobs were to nurse me back to health with the assistance of the animal-shelter staff and to help find me a permanent home.

After careful instructions from the shelter staff, my new foster parents took me to their home. I stepped into the house and discovered that they already had three white, fluffy dogs and two cats. I was nervous. *Would I fit in with them? Would they accept me?*

My foster mom tucked me in every night, making sure I was comfortable before I fell asleep. She assured me that they would find me a permanent home. I wanted to believe her. My foster mom talked to me sweetly and softly. Though I had never experienced such affection, I still longed for a place to call home and a family of my own.

I really liked my new foster dad. He helped me to heal. He picked the maggots off me when no one else would or could. "I can handle it. I have a strong stomach," he would say.

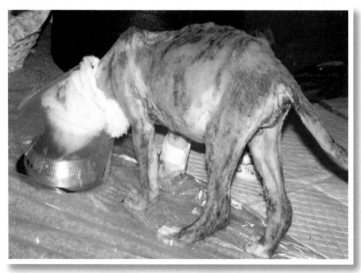

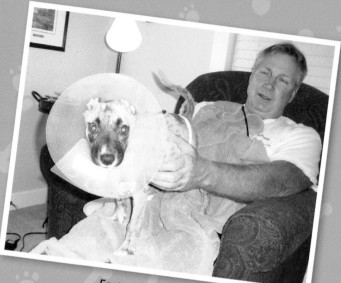

Foster Dad Bob Wall

Foster Mom Roberta Wall

 22

My foster mom had to work a lot, so my foster dad took over my care. In the beginning, he drove me to and from the shelter daily so that I could continue my burn treatments. Later he took me every other day. Eventually those trips tapered off to twice a week. He always cared for my needs without complaint.

The people at the animal shelter continued to care for me as well. When my foster dad brought me in, the shelter staff bathed me. They provided medical treatment that I was unable to receive at home. For most of my treatments, I was anesthetized because the pain would have been unbearable. It was amazing to see how everyone pulled together to ensure my recovery. All of this was done for me, a poor dog.

My medical expenses were high. It would have been a burden on the shelter if people hadn't stepped up and donated, so the shelter began to raise money to pay for my expenses. Many people

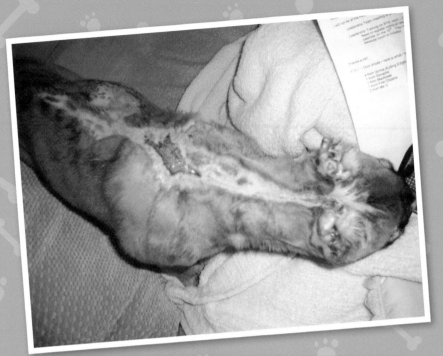

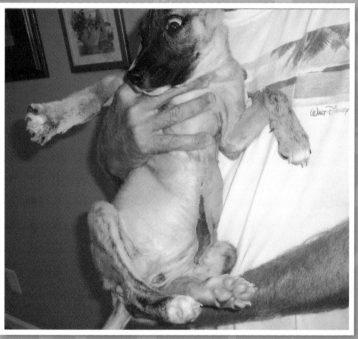

24

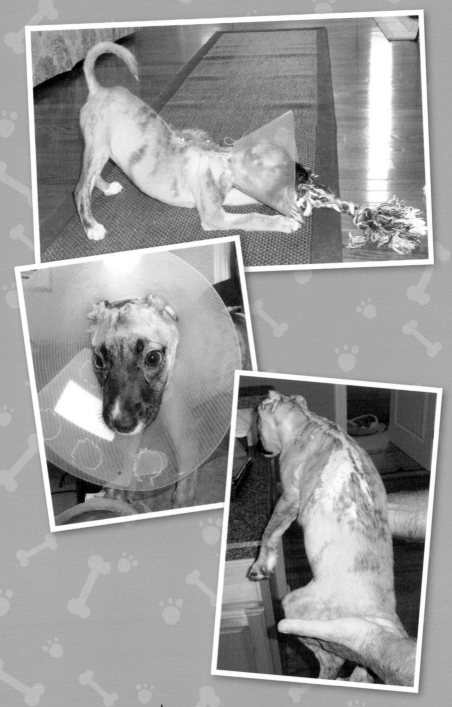

from all around the area gave what they could. People were intrigued by my story and wanted to help. What a blessing this was to both the shelter and me. In fact, even more money came in than was needed. The extra money went into Susie's Miracle Fund, a fund started to help other abused animals.

—m—

Life in my foster home was becoming normal. I was beginning to fit right in. Although I had disrupted their lives, my foster parents never complained. I was getting better and they realized it was time to start looking for my permanent home. Life was changing for all of us, but it was definitely better for me.

My foster parents had to keep me separated from their other animals so they gave me my very own special room on the second floor of their home. I really couldn't be around the other dogs, although sometimes I longed for their company. I had not yet gotten all of my shots, and my burns still required care. This special room brought the comfort and safety that I needed at that time.

My foster parents also had to build a fenced-in area for me inside so that I could play without getting hurt. Sometimes dogs need to be protected from themselves. After all, I wasn't

just a wounded dog. I was also an energetic puppy that needed boundaries.

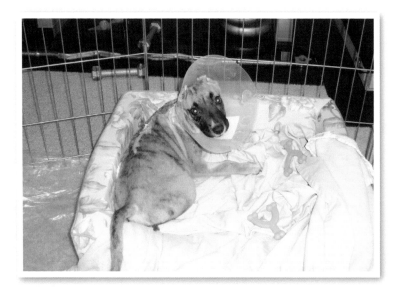

Lots of people wanted to visit me while I was in their home.
"We want to see the burned dog!" they would exclaim. At first,
I was cautious. But I soon realized that people were just curi-
ous. They brought love with them. I began to feel so special, so
esteemed. I was becoming a hot topic in town.

I enjoyed it when adults came, but I especially loved children who stopped by. After my foster parents explained how
to touch and speak to me, the children got on their hands
and knees to imitate my stance. They giggled and asked questions. Sometimes I could see the concern for me in their eyes.
The human touch became something I craved and no lon-

ger feared. The human voice that once brought fright now soothed me.

Of all of the visitors who stopped by, my favorite was actually another dog—a little Boston terrier. Although he was much smaller than me, we both had the same amount of energy. We chased each other and played. He accepted me for what I was. His eyes seemed to overlook my wounds. I was just a playful pup like him.

Chapter 4
A New Face

My foster parents had a vacation planned, and they really needed it. *But what were they going to do with me while they were gone?* After all, I was not the easiest animal to look after. I wasn't a pet they could just drop off at someone's house for a week. I needed continual care from someone who would follow their strict orders. *But who would come and stay at their home for one week, give me all of the attention that they did, and do it with a willing heart?*

After much thought, my foster parents found someone special. She had the same passion for animals and concerns for me that they did. She was willing to do all that was necessary

 29

to care for me. She was even going to drive me to and from the animal shelter just like my foster dad did. Her name was Donna, and it was as if God had sent her. Later we'd all see how our crossing paths were part of God's plans for both of us.

When Donna first came to stay with me, I discovered that she was funny. Talking was definitely her gift, and she did a lot of it. She shared with me how adorable and extraordinary I was. She had heard my story from the media. How terribly sorry and angry she was about my situation! I liked to listen to her talk. She had a really heavy Southern accent and jumped from one conversation to the next with such enthusiasm. She was fun to be around.

Donna owned her own hair salon. She was a people person, and she also had so much compassion for animals. Most importantly, she loved God with all of her heart. Donna and her husband Roy had taken in lost or abused animals before.

While she was with me for the week of their vacation, Donna paid close attention to the detailed instructions left by my foster parents. We bonded during that week and during our trips to the animal shelter. I never once felt like I was a bother to her. In fact, I knew that I became her priority that week. She rushed home after work just to sit with me and watch movies in my own special room upstairs. She often rubbed my head and my back, trying to ease the pain, while we spent time together.

Chapter 5
A Forever Home?

Donna definitely liked to show affection. At least ten times a day, she grabbed my face and laid a wet kiss right on me. She told me how beautiful and sweet I was, and then she kissed me again. How tender she was.

Because I needed exercise daily, as all dogs do, she took me downstairs to play. She threw golf balls around the house, encouraging me to chase them. I loved that game. While we were playing a game of cat and mouse one day, I got so excited that I actually opened my mouth and barked! The only noises that I had made since my abuse had been the ones of agony and pain. Donna got so excited that she made a phone call to my foster parents just to share the news. They all rejoiced at this audible sign of recovery.

Another event that occurred during that week was the visit from Roy, Donna's husband. More and more, I realized how enjoyable humans could be. He reminded me so much of my foster dad. He got down on the floor and played with me, rubbed my head and back, and spoke kind words as well.

I really enjoyed this couple and wondered if they would become candidates to adopt me. They were so much fun and I could tell they really liked me. Donna was very careful with me and made sure I took my medication all week. She tucked me in every night, and I saw tears in her eyes as she rubbed my scars and talked softly saying, "You poor baby, how could someone be so mean to you? There is no way that you deserved this. No animal should have to endure something like this." One night as we were bonding, she shared with me that we had a lot in common. But she didn't go into what she meant. She just cried as she rubbed me.

Soon enough, vacation was over and my foster parents returned home. The search for a "forever home" for me began. My foster parents were only temporary parents. I had to be moved to a permanent home. My foster parents already had three dogs and two cats. I was in the other animals' territory, and I practically dominated their lives. Because dogs are territorial animals and I was on their turf, I had to be placed in a new home.

More than 60 families wanted to adopt me, but finding the right home was going to be challenging. Neither the animal shelter nor my foster parents were going to let me go to just anyone. I had many scars and no ears. And I was getting bigger and found it harder to contain my excitement in a lot of situations. To help me control my impulses and teach me how to act like a well-behaved dog, my foster mom had a trainer come in and work with me. I was really making progress. She wanted

to ensure that my progress would continue. In addition, I needed lots of care to guarantee my full recovery.

The search came down to just two or three people. Because of the breed I am—part pit bull—many people were reluctant to adopt me. This breed causes mixed feelings in the community. Often people think of pit bulls as vicious and dangerous. However, many owners train pit bulls to be gentle, well-behaved, and simply protective. Either way, it was a significant issue when finding a new family to love me.

Chapter 6
Weekends at Donna's

The search was beginning to weigh on my foster parents. They had invested so much—including their time, love, and money—in me. Sending me off to just anyone was not going to go well for any of us. During this time of searching, Donna continued to be a part of my life. Often my foster mom took me to her business meetings, and I would see Donna there. I would immediately run up to Donna and hope for some more of those kisses that she loved to give. How I loved to give her wet kisses back!

There were other times when I would see Donna, too. My foster mom and Donna were becoming friends. They shared

 35

both a love for animals and concerns about cruelty to animals, so I would often cross paths with Donna not only on weekdays, but also on Saturdays and Sundays as well.

Eventually Donna wanted to help my foster parents by taking me to her house on the weekends. At first, I was unsure of the new environment. Donna and Roy already owned one dog, Baby Girl, not to mention the seven cats living there as well. (Dogs have owners. Cats have staff.) It had been hard trying to bond with the white, fluffy lapdogs at my foster home. But a house with so many cats…?

While at Donna's house, I would lie around and relax in her large, fenced-in backyard. I also had the freedom to run around and be a puppy without the possibility of escaping. Even if the fence had not been there, I am sure that I would have stayed put. Who would want to leave such safety and comfort?

Baby Girl and I began to bond as well. I ran around the yard, chasing her until she couldn't run anymore. I was a puppy with all of that puppy energy. I enjoyed every minute of it. Donna and Roy sat outside and watched me play, encouraging me to run around and get all of my energy out. I needed that support. For so long I had been carefully supervised. I had not been allowed to run freely and play without the fear of getting hurt. Oh, how good it felt to run, jump, and play!

 36

Susie and Baby Girl

Our bonds grew stronger and stronger every weekend. Donna treated me as if I were one of her pets. *Would she become a candidate to be my new master?* I was hopeful.

After each weekend with Donna, I returned to my foster home, hoping that Donna would see the need to bring me to her home for good. I already knew that I liked her very much and that she was the one for me. I could envision us as a family since we had special bonds. She sometimes continued to share with me that we both had so much in common, and for some odd reason, I sensed that we did. She still didn't explain what she meant.

I thought that the weekend trips could really turn out for the best. I could become a part of her family in ways I had never known. I began to tell myself that this was going to be a good thing. I was hopeful.

After one weekend visit, I overheard several phone conversations between my foster mom and Donna. Donna really wanted to take me in, and secretly I was hoping for that. However, their main concern was how I would get along with the seven cats. Although Donna and Roy had hearts for animals, taking me in was another addition to an already-full house.

Apparently there were only two possible families left, and my foster mom was very concerned. The end of the search was near, but there were several loose ends still left untied.

 38

Chapter 7
A Trial Run at Donna's

I had lived with my foster family for three months and had
gone to Donna's on the weekends. After much thought and
discussion, my foster mom, my trainer, and Donna decided
that it was time for me to do a trial run at Donna and Roy's
house to see how we interacted. They wanted to get a feel
for my possible new environment. *Was there enough room for
another dog? Would I interact well with the other animals already
living there? Could Donna handle me and follow through with
my treatments and training?* These were all questions that my
trainer, my foster mom, and Donna needed answered.

 39

So my trainer, my foster mom, and Donna all agreed that Donna should take me home the following weekend. I was already used to her home and the environment, but now I was growing into my full-grown weight and size. I wasn't little anymore. And I was very energetic. One way or the other, any looming questions would soon be answered.

When my foster parents and I arrived at Donna's house, I wasn't sure how this would end. *Would everyone be for or against this adoption?* My foster mom already had high hopes. When we entered the house, I immediately saw Donna. With her sweet, loving words, she called to me. And she had such a soft, gentle touch with her hands that she seemed almost angelic. I approached her, and she began to rub my head and stroke the scars on my back that were now healed.

My foster parents already knew that Donna would be the perfect one for me. But everyone needed to be sure, and Donna wanted her husband Roy to be convinced as well. That was not hard to accomplish. As we all sat down together, God intervened. It was clear that Donna was perfect for me, I was perfect for her, and Roy was on board as well. They had found a new home for me. And I would be able to continue to see my foster parents. What a perfect solution!

Chapter 8
Moving Day

After Donna and Roy signed my adoption papers on December 8, 2009, and met with the workers from the animal shelter, my official moving day arrived. It was a bittersweet time for my foster parents. They had valued me above all, and now they had to let me go. The ride to Donna's was one filled with sadness and joy.

It was early on a December Sunday afternoon when we pulled up. My foster parents unloaded my cage, my toys, and my clothes. No more weekend visits to Donna. I was permanently a part of this home. When we entered the house, Donna ran over, picked me up, and gave me a big kiss. I knew by the

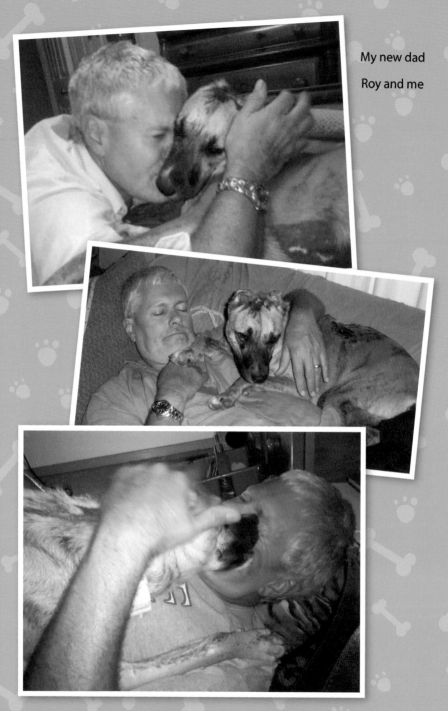

My new dad
Roy and me

42

way she looked into my eyes that love and compassion were at the very center of her being. She spoke with the kindness of a mother. From that very moment, I knew she never would permit anything bad to happen to me again if she could prevent it. I darted in every direction and jumped on every piece of furniture. I was so excited to be back—excited to be home.

They opened the back door so I could play outside, and again, I ran all over the place. There was so much energy bottled up inside me that I even surprised myself. Baby Girl came outside to join me, and we began to play like never before. *Yes, this new life was going to be just perfect,* I thought. Just then, my foster parents joined me outside. They pulled me close and whispered their good-byes. I knew I would see them again… but when?

Within minutes, I learned that Donna was a master who was on the go. I was just along for the ride. She had planned for Baby Girl and me to be in the Christmas parade in Jamestown. I was going to represent the animal shelter on a float, so she dressed us in our Santa suits and we were on our way. We had so much fun that day. As my mom tucked me in for bed in my crate that night, she said, "You now have a place to call home. Don't worry. I will always protect you." Somehow I knew she really meant it.

—m—

Each night after that, as soon as Donna tucked me in for bed I would wiggle my way out of my crate. I'd climb into her lap for one last kiss and rub. Even though I was bigger than Baby Girl and all of the cats, she always seemed to make enough room for me.

One night as my mom went to bed she looked at me in the crate. I gave her that little cry that asked if I could sleep with them. I think she felt sorry for me. She told my dad that since Baby Girl was sleeping with them, I should too. I jumped into their bed between them. The next morning I woke up cuddled by my dad. I realized that I felt safe because his arms were so comforting. He was beginning to heal my fear of men. My first male owner had placed such cruel hands upon me.

He had spoken angry words and had kicked me around. My dad dimmed those memories, replacing them with warm, new memories of the gentle hands of a true master. My dad also restored my loyalty to humans by wiping out my fear and pain. In their place, he showed me gentleness and trust.

—⟋⟋—

My mom was so excited that we got to spend our first Christmas together. She told me that I was her Christmas present. She told my dad she didn't want anything for Christmas but me with a big red bow around my neck. She put up the Christmas tree while Baby Girl and I chased each other all over the house. We had the best Christmas all together as one happy family. On Christmas Day she dressed Baby Girl and me up in Christmas outfits and took lots of pictures. And she had Christmas presents for us to open. That day was really special.

—⟋⟋—

Luckily for me, in my new home I didn't have to do lots of adjusting. I knew the boundaries, and I fit right in. However, there were still some minor changes that I had to make. For example, Rule Number One: no chasing the cats. Baby Girl loved chasing them, so I simply followed her example. I learned fast that following the leader wasn't always such a good idea.

 46

I began to feel out my place in the home. One night, while Baby Girl and I were playing, I let out a growl. You should have seen the look on my mom's face. Evidently, that growl terrified her; she did not know what to make of it. She became fearful of me. She cried herself to sleep that night.

The next morning I overheard a phone call that she made to my foster parents. "I just don't know if I can do this!" Donna exclaimed. "What if I made the wrong choice?"

This couldn't be happening. Donna had to know that I was meant to be in her home.

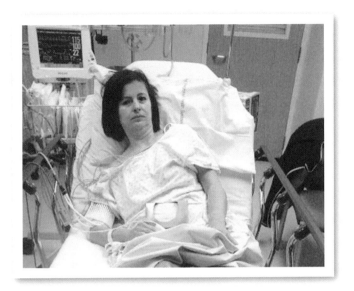

Chapter 9
Memories of a Pit Bull

I came to realize that Donna had every right to be afraid. From the bits and pieces I could gather from their phone conversation, I learned that Donna had been attacked by a pit bull the year before. I am part pit bull and part shepherd. No wonder my growling had scared her. It was then that I realized what Donna had meant when she had kept saying, "You and I have so much in common."

———ш———

It seems that at one time, her neighbors next door had owned a pit bull. For almost five years, the dog had been

 49

chained outside, neglected, and underfed. One day, those neighbors moved, leaving the dog behind after finding out that the place they'd moved to didn't allow pets. The neighbor asked Donna if she would find the dog a home. He knew my mom felt sorry for the dog and didn't want to see it suffer any longer. Instead of calling animal control, she decided to care for it herself. Her plans were to clean the dog up and find it a good home.

Each day she went over to the neighbor's house, placed a bowl of dog food in its doghouse, and left. For days she did this without any trouble. One night she had the dog in her yard and was feeding it and loving it. She wanted to keep the dog in the yard all night, but Roy wouldn't allow it. He was scared of the dog. My mom took it back, and that night in its doghouse as she put down bedding for it, the dog even kissed her on the face. My mom later said, "Looking back on it, the dog could have killed me then. God was definitely looking out for me." My mom had no fear of dogs.

One morning in October 2008, during a routine visit to the neighbor's house, the dog attacked her from behind. He threw her to the ground and clamped onto her leg with his vicious jaws. With one swift kick from her left leg, she was able to kick the dog off her. But then, he became more aggressive and tried to seize her throat. Donna said, "I went into shock. I just knew the dog was going to kill me, and my family would find me lying out here torn to pieces." Her adrenaline kicked in. As the dog lunged for her throat, she grabbed him by the throat and held on to his collar. The dog started biting on her hand, but she knew it was either her hand or her throat.

Suddenly God intervened and Donna heard a voice say, "Throw and roll." And that's just what she did. With almost-supernatural strength, she was able to throw the dog off her and roll just out of the reach of its chain. She jumped up and gasped when she saw how badly her leg was injured. Her hand was also bleeding. She knew she was in trouble and had to get help fast. She ran to a neighbor's house about a fourth of a mile down the street, praying the whole way. She felt like she was about to pass out from the trauma and the loss of so much blood. As she beat on the neighbor's door, she fell to the ground and went into a state of shock.

Donna ended up in the emergency room with about 50 stitches in her leg and tubes running out in every direction. The hospital staff had to monitor her closely because of the fear of infection. She heard the doctors say, "You are lucky to be alive. Most people don't survive an attack like that. And if they do, they usually lose an arm or a leg." Donna realized that she had experienced a miracle. She was a survivor.

As she lay in that hospital bed, she couldn't help but cry as she thought about the poor dog that had attacked her. He would be the one that paid the ultimate price with his life. And he'd be stigmatized as the dog that attacked a human.

The pit bull had to be kept at the local animal shelter for ten days to check for rabies, since his former owner didn't get him his shots. The animal had to be watched closely for any signs of rabies. If the dog had showed any signs, then Donna would have had to get all of the rabies shots. After ten days, the dog's test came back normal.

Donna tried to go on with life as usual. She walked on crutches for two months. She went back and forth to the emergency room so that doctors could check her leg for any infection. She had to be out of work for over a month, and when she returned, she had to sit on a stool to cut hair. For months, Donna walked with a limp and couldn't walk fast.

As Donna began to heal physically, she still had to heal emotionally. She found herself crying a lot and developing a great deal of fear of dogs. One day while she was visiting a friend, her fear became so bad that she began to shake. She asked her friend to remove their dog. Every time she was around a big dog, her body trembled. She even got a little nervous being around her own dog Baby Girl. Fear was taking over her life.

My mom's attack had happened only a year before she met me, so all of that fear was deep down inside her. I was the first dog that she had gotten close to besides Baby Girl. She said that there was something about me that inspired her and helped her overcome her own fear. Every time she got around me, she felt inspiration and strength. She said, "If that little puppy can overcome her fear of humans after what happened to her, I can overcome my fear of dogs."

Donna also said, "God told me to adopt you and that He had special plans for us." My mom said we were a match made in heaven. We both had been wrongfully attacked: me by a human and her by a dog. We both had to learn the powerful message of love, hope, and forgiveness.

So it seemed both of us experienced life-changing, traumatic events within the past year. God's plans for us were beginning to unfold.

With a great deal of guidance and prayer, my mom knew that she had to keep me. One answer was simple: she and I needed more training. She needed to be taught how to command me. Dogs are always willing to obey a loving, yet assertive master. We were both ready for our training as a team to begin.

My new master continually reassured me that I was not going anywhere. She told me over and over how much she loved me and that she was willing to care for my every need. "There is no turning back," she would say. Although she had some fears to deal with, Donna decided that she was no longer going to be chained by them. Donna said that God told her to adopt me and that, through our experiences, He was going to heal both of us.

Something sparked inside me. All of the pieces were falling into place. God had brought us together for one purpose: to heal each other!

Donna had always been an animal lover, helping wounded or lost animals whenever possible. But the dog attack had squelched that desire in her. God wanted to restore her love for animals. We had something in common, too, because I had been attacked by a man, Donna by a dog. Through Donna's human touch and care, I have learned to trust and to be loyal once again, just as God created me to be.

 54

Chapter 10
Learning to Trust

It has been over two years since I moved into my new home. Much has changed since then. Although you can still see scars on both my mom and me, our inner pain is a thing of the past. In addition, Donna and I trust each other. We are letting go our fears—hers of animals and mine of humans. Fears won't control us any longer.

Mom and I took a summer vacation together at the beach. She was excited for me, because I had never been at a beach before. She assured me I would love it. Unfortunately animals could not be on the beach at that time of year. We had been invited by my foster parents, and it was fun to see them again and to hang out with their white, fluffy dogs. When we arrived, I was so excited. I had never seen anything like that. My mom took me out on the beach, and I ran and ran. I loved jumping in the waves, rolling in the sand, and chasing the birds.

I was disappointed that I couldn't be on the beach all day every day. My mom was unhappy about that too, so she decided to get up early every morning and sneak me out at 6:00. Then I would have time on the beach before the sun came up and we were spotted. Since it was my only daily time to go out, I was sure to wake her up. She is *not* a morning person but she loved me so much that she got up. After we spent time on the beach, she walked me around the park so I wouldn't be stuck in the room all day.

At night I enjoyed looking over the balcony and listening to the sounds of the waves. All week my mom took pictures of me playing in the sand and chasing the birds. My mom assured me that she, Baby Girl, and I would go to a beach that allowed pets in the future.

—⬿—

Both Donna and Roy recognized that God had a mighty purpose for me and that I had been spared to fulfill it. My mom and I have been out in public, visiting churches, schools, and other organizations. In the beginning, we helped at fundraisers for Susie's Miracle Fund. Now that we have our own nonprofit organization, we no longer have time to help with that too. Donna has shared our stories, focusing on the fact that we were brought together for a divine purpose. During visits, she wants people to learn that fear should not be an enemy that binds us. She says, "If we face our fears, we can watch them disappear."

We also have started the Susie's Hope™ nonprofit organization. Through the organization, we spread the message of love, hope, and forgiveness. We are working to inspire and educate others not to accept animal abuse and neglect. We teach children animal safety and how to properly take care of their pets. My mom hopes that by educating these children, they won't grow up to harm animals and then turn on people.

We have continued with my obedience training on a weekly basis. Through this training, my mom and I have bonded well. I love her so much, and I gaze at her all of the time with my big brown eyes. Mom loves it when I do that. My trainer, Ally Thomas, has taught my mom how to teach me to do many tricks like riding a skateboard. Then my mom taught me. I like jumping through hoops, going through agility courses, and knowing all of the basic commands. I love making my mom proud of me. You can read more about Ally on page 97.

I have passed the Canine Good Citizen course and test. That means that I am certified, and it allows me to go into schools and nursing homes. To find out more about this certification test, please read page 99. Next I will get certified as a therapy dog.

Media people have been tracking our story and my road to recovery. People from all around have come to see me, the burned dog. Others have become animal-shelter sponsors and supporters of our Susie's Hope™ program. We made the headlines in the newspaper, and we have a Facebook page about Susie's Law and the legislation that now has more than 34,000 fans. We also have a second Facebook page called Susie's Hope™ that explains about spreading our message.

Now I have my very own stuffed animal that looks just like me. A production team is in development of a feature-length film about our stories. The movie will be produced by the Susie's Hope™ nonprofit organization, which will benefit from its proceeds. My mom hopes that I can play my part somewhere in the movie. Maybe I will see you from the big screen one day.

Chapter 11
Our Court Date

Three months after I was found, the perpetrator of my abuse was caught through a Crimestoppers tip. A couple of weeks before our court date, my mom met with the police detective and the prosecuting attorney on the case.

The prosecuting attorney said, "Do you know that there is no jail time for what happened to Susie?" My mom was shocked.

She said, "This is not right! We must do something about it."

On March 1, 2010, Donna and I had our day in court. The day the trial began, my mom and my foster mom were ready.

They had TV crews there as well as many of my supporters. They wanted to make the statement that no one will tolerate this. I had to face the man who abused me. My mom and my foster parents were right by my side supporting me.

When my abuser walked into the courtroom in his chains, I was sleeping beside my mom. I raised my head and looked right at him. But he was not going to bother me. I just lay back down. I am a survivor.

The courtroom was packed. Cameras were snapping. People watched my response to him. My mom said that my reaction to my abuser that day made her realize that an animal

truly lives in the moment and not in the past. She also learned just how forgiving an animal can be. Later she said, "If people could be that forgiving, how much greater our world would be."

After our court day, people asked her how she felt toward my abuser. And she responded, "I couldn't help but feel pity for him." She also told them that if dogs can forgive people, then humans should forgive as well. *Forgiveness* doesn't mean that

you agree with what the person did; it means that you move past it to focus on the positive things in life. My mom forgave him, especially after seeing how I had for-given him. She said that if we refuse to forgive, we will be-come bitter, angry persons no better than the abuser.

As the prosecuting attorney began building his case, he asked my foster dad to walk me right up in front of the judge to show him how badly I was burned. The judge took one look at me and said, "I am sorry that under North Carolina structured-sentencing guidelines, there is no jail time for this. There is only probation for first-time offenders." The judge did not have the option to give my abuser jail time for the cruelty charge, a Class I felony, which was the lowest level of felony.

While the prosecuting attorney gave his closing statement, Donna was in tears as she heard for the first time the entire story of what happened to me. Everyone in that courtroom seemed shocked as he shared what happened that night. My abuser had told the attorney that his excuse for burning me was that he awoke in the middle of the night to find the puppy licking their one-month-old baby in the face. He got angry, snapped, and flew into a rage. He grabbed the dog by its fur and dragged it outside. Then he grabbed a barbecue lighter and pressed its button to pour lighter fluid all over the dog's body. After holding her down and beating her for about 15 minutes, he set the dog on fire with a match. He said he tried to put the fire out, but she ran into the woods. Everyone in the courtroom was furious. They could not believe that this happened to me.

My abuser was motionless and unresponsive. He did not speak to the court except to answer questions from the judge about his plea. His lawyer said he was deeply remorseful for his actions. His client snapped and couldn't control his actions or his emotions. He had no excuses for that.

My mom said she wondered what he was thinking that day. *Did he realize how horrible what he did to me was, or did he even understand what he did?* My abuser's mom showed up for court but didn't talk to anyone afterwards. Donna had read in the newspaper that his mom had said that she had raised a good child who was crying out for help. She had stated that he had suffered from mental illness caused by watching his eight-year-old brother get struck and killed by a car when he was seven.

Those in court said that my case was one of the worst they had seen in Guilford County in recent memory. They found it hard to believe that I was tortured the way I was and lived. Citizens of Guilford County realized that day just how minimal the penalties were for cruelty to animals.

The man who did this to me only got four to five months of probation for felony cruelty to animals. He got eight months for the burning of personal property (I was the personal property). That meant that you could have burned your neighbor's

 67

couch and gotten more time than you could have gotten for burning an animal. That was what really made everyone so upset. My abuser was sentenced to some jail time for other crimes that he committed, but not for what he did to me.

The assistant district attorney asked everyone in the courtroom to stand up on my behalf. At that moment at least half of the people in the courtroom stood up. My mom was so proud that everyone turned out to support me. After our day in court, my foster parents and my mom decided to do something about this injustice.

Christopher L. Parrish

Assistant District Attorney for the State of North Carolina in the 18th Prosecutorial District

Assistant District Attorney Parrish shared, "On the day Susie's assailant was sentenced, I asked that Susie appear with me in order to illustrate to the court the horrific nature of the offense. It is unfortunate that such a terrible event must take place to facilitate a needed adjustment in the law."

Chapter 12
The New Law

My foster parents, Donna, Susie's Team, thousands of Guilford County residents, and I wanted to stop cruelty to animals. We wanted to create stricter laws for those who abuse their pets. *Susie's Law* was our first endeavor. Before Susie's Law, penalties for animal abuse were minor. First we had to learn about the laws for felony cruelty to animals in place at that time and how the criminal justice system worked.

Susie's Team rallied all over the state of North Carolina to get people in each county on board. In March 2010, we started going door-to-door in different counties asking citizens to

 69

send letters and E-mails to the state-capitol building in Raleigh. We even sent postcards with my picture on them to our legislators asking for stiffer penalties for animal abuse. Countless letters began to pour in from North Carolina citizens. Concerned citizens also began lobbying legislators to increase the penalties for such crimes so judges would have the option to give jail time.

The team presented a resolution before the Greensboro City Council as well as to the Guilford County Commissioners. Both groups voted yes to the resolution. Then we were off to Raleigh to change the law.

After hearing my story, North Carolina State Senator Don Vaughan got busy. He worked alongside us to make some major changes to the laws. Senator Vaughan wrote the bill for all abused animals and me. He said, "Let's call it Susie's Law." I was so excited that the bill was named after me!

Donna and Susie's Team took me to Raleigh for the House session. My mom walked me around the room so legislators could see my scars and the results of my abuse. The bill passed unanimously in the North Carolina House in May 2010 and in the North Carolina Senate in June.

In June 2010 we went to Raleigh to the North Carolina executive mansion's shady back lawn for the bill-signing ceremony. My mom and I met Governor Perdue privately before the signing of the bill. She hugged my mom and thanked her for adopting me and giving other animals a voice. And

she shook my paw and rubbed my head. I could feel her sympathy for me. I got to meet Governor Perdue's two dogs Zipper and Dosie. I liked them very much.

I had dressed up for the occasion with my nails painted pink and my pearls around my neck. Governor Perdue said, "Susie is a true Southerner in her pearls." That day was the start of my trademark precious pearls around my neck.

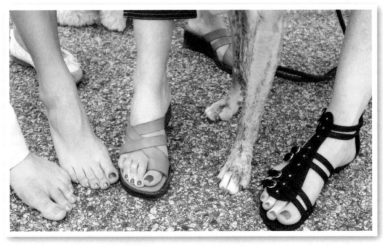

 71

That was a great day for me, surrounded by the media. Governor Perdue made sure my mom and I were right by her side for the signing of the bill. During its signing, Governor Perdue said, "I can't imagine what I would have done or what I would have said or how angry and hurt I would have been if somebody had done to our dogs what was done to Susie. I think it is absolutely unacceptable." And guess what! My paw print is on the bill. How awesome is that?

Susie's Law became effective in December 2010. It allows for jail time of up to ten months for first-time offenders. The judge has the option to give the jail time. Felony cruelty to animals was elevated from a Class I felony to a Class H felony. The Class A1 misdemeanor was elevated to a Class H felony as well. That means that people who intentionally starve their animals to death will get jail time also. This is a terrific start for the protection of all animals.

GENERAL ASSEMBLY OF NORTH CAROLINA
SESSION 2009

06-18-10A09:08 RCVD

SENATE BILL 254
RATIFIED BILL

AN ACT TO INCREASE THE PENALTY FOR THE MALICIOUS ABUSE, TORTURE, OR KILLING OF AN ANIMAL.

The General Assembly of North Carolina enacts:

SECTION 1. G.S. 14-360(a1) reads as rewritten:
"(a1)   If any person shall maliciously kill, or cause or procure to be killed, any animal by intentional deprivation of necessary sustenance, that person shall be guilty of a ~~Class A1 misdemeanor.~~ Class H felony."
SECTION 2. G.S. 14-360(b) reads as rewritten:
"(b)   If any person shall maliciously torture, mutilate, maim, cruelly beat, disfigure, poison, or kill, or cause or procure to be tortured, mutilated, maimed, cruelly beaten, disfigured, poisoned, or killed, any animal, every such offender shall for every such offense be guilty of a ~~Class I~~ Class H felony. However, nothing in this section shall be construed to increase the penalty for cockfighting provided for in G.S. 14-362."
SECTION 3.   This act becomes effective December 1, 2010, and applies to offenses committed on or after that date.
In the General Assembly read three times and ratified this the 17th day of June, 2010.

_____
Walter H. Dalton
President of the Senate

_____
William L. Wainwright
Speaker Pro Tempore of the House of Representatives

_____
Beverly E. Perdue
Governor

ved _1:46 p_.m. this __23rd__ day of __June__, 2010 ·

Susie's Law

 73

Left to Right: House Representative Pricey Harrison, House Representative Maggie Jeffus, Senator Don Vaughan, *(behind)* House Representative Laura Wiley, House Representative Alma Adams

Governor Bev Perdue signed the bill, which includes Susie's paw print.

Susie's Team

Chapter 13
Our Future

Without God, none of these doors would have been opened. Without God, Donna never would have survived the pit bull's attack. And she never would have had the courage to adopt me. Without God, I would have died all alone in the park. I never would have found out my purpose in life.

Donna and I are being trained to minister to burn victims, cancer patients, and victims of violence and abuse. I hope to become a therapy dog in hospital burn units. Donna and I tell the story of two miracles—human and animal.

I am Susie. I am a survivor.
I am the voice for all abused
and neglected animals.
Together Donna and I are
spreading the message of love,
hope, and forgiveness.

Epilogue

Susie is living a very happy and fulfilling life. She and Donna travel throughout North Carolina doing fund-raising events, speaking engagements, and programs to educate children in schools. She loves going to work with her mom and greeting the customers as they walk in each day.

Susie and Baby Girl are the best of friends, and she loves chasing Baby Girl around the backyard. She also lives with eight cats that have become her pack. She loves all of them. Susie has two other special friends, Bailey and Phoenix, that she loves to hang out with. Susie, Bailey, and Phoenix share

 78

something in common and can relate to each other. All three dogs were burned. Susie and Phoenix were burned intentionally, and Bailey was burned accidentally. You can read their stories at the end of this book. Look for them on pages 89 (Phoenix) and 91 (Bailey).

Susie, Phoenix, and Bailey travel together with their owners, Donna Lawrence, Deborah Hodges, and Keely Greene. They all work together as a team to educate and to inspire others to help put an end to animal abuse and cruelty. If you want to join their efforts in helping to stop animal abuse and neglect, read more about the Susie's Hope™ nonprofit organization on this book's flap. And join us at www.susieshope.com.

Susie's Law is often in the media spotlight on TV news shows, on Facebook, in magazines, and in newspapers. Citizens in other states are pursuing similar legislation for their states.

A Heartfelt Message from Donna Lawrence

Two years ago, my husband and I adopted Susie. She had been badly abused and left to die. Susie has forever changed my life. She has opened my eyes to the truth about animal abuse and the epidemic it has become. I am very concerned about the welfare of all animals, and it truly breaks my heart to see any animal mistreated or abused.

Every morning I look into the face of a dog that was beaten and burned beyond belief. I can't imagine someone being so cruel to a helpless animal that only wants to give love and respect. Almost every day we hear of animals being abandoned, tortured, and abused. There is a significant body of research that shows that a person who abuses or neglects animals will do

the same to children. When people who torture or abuse animals go unpunished, that opens a wide door for future criminal activity.

In December 2010, Susie's Law was enacted to strengthen North Carolina's cruelty-to-animals statute. This is a terrific beginning for protecting our animals. We can all help in many other ways such as reporting suspected cases of abuse, volunteering at the local animal shelter, adopting an abandoned or fostered or rescued pet, and supporting the local shelter or animal-rescue groups. We must continue advocating for stiffer laws and better pet licensing, as well as promoting spaying and neutering in our communities. Every year too many animals are starved, abused, neglected, and abandoned. We can get angry and bitter, or we can find a way to make things better.

I appreciate everything that was done on the behalf of my sweet Susie. I know that God brought her into my life for a reason. There were many people involved in saving her life, as well as in nurturing her back to health. Susie survived because of many reasons, one being that she was a strong-willed born leader, which worked in her favor. She also survived due to the powerful influences of everyone who acted on her behalf.

Thanks to Susie and all of the caring North Carolina citizens who love and respect animals, animals now have a voice. God works in mysterious ways, and he can take something negative and turn it into something positive and beautiful. Susie was wrongfully attacked and paid the price for other abused animals in North Carolina. Now justice can be served and animals can be saved. I don't think Susie would trade her life now for the past. And if she had to do it all over again to be where she is now, I think she would.

One thing that God showed me through all of this is that we cannot allow hate toward people to enter our hearts. We hate the crime, not the person. People have to be punished for their wrongdoings toward animals as well as toward other people. Forgiveness doesn't mean people don't pay for their crimes, but forgiveness can set us free from the bondage within and from the prison we live in within ourselves when we choose not to let go of wrongful actions. When we don't forgive and allow hate in our hearts, then we are no better than the person who committed the crime. Susie's abuser is obviously a young man who is hurting from within. I never allowed bitterness and resentment toward him into my heart. I was angry about what he did, but never at him personally.

Everything happens in our lives for a reason, and with God's assistance, Susie and I helped to turn things around for the good of all animals. I have had so many people come up to me and tell me how Susie and I have changed their lives for the good. We have helped them both forgive and let go of bitter feelings toward others. In the end, that is what life is all about: helping our fellow man as well as the animals that God put here and gave us dominion over.

Susie and I came together for a reason and

for such a time as this. We were meant to be together. Our similar experiences allowed us both to go from being victims to living a victorious life. I forgave an animal for my wrongful attack, and she forgave a human for her wrongful attack. Forgiveness will bring healing to our hearts and will allow us to move forward for whatever God has in store for us.

~Donna

Susie and I both say
to her abuser.
"You are forgiven."

85

Susie's

Photo Album

Susie's Special Friends
Phoenix and Deborah

Sometimes in life we feel like we live day to day doing the same old things. I had thought about fostering a pet for our animal shelter because I needed more in my life. Then I heard about the puppy that had been burned by four boys. Instantly I had the desire to do something for him. His name is Phoenix.

I agreed to foster him until he was ready for his permanent home. So the journey has begun for many such animals. I had to take him to the Guilford County Animal Shelter for his skin treatments every day seven days a week for seven weeks. This poor puppy had body wraps that had to be removed every day so his wounds could be cleaned. Fridays were much tougher, because the old, dead skin had to be removed. As Phoenix grew, it became harder for him to walk because so much of his skin had been burned that he had had to have skin grafts done.

I watched him sleeping many nights with tears in my eyes. I could tell he was uncomfortable at times. He had to wear a plastic collar for a few months. Sleeping in that collar was no fun. It may have bothered me more than it did him.

He is the most lovable dog, but how can that be? I truly believe that unconditional love and time can heal the physical and emotional wounds and pain of even the most-abused pets. Phoenix is living proof. I have learned so much from him. If he can forgive and love unconditionally, then I can too.

It was a long journey but once again he could hold his head high and life went on. As I share this horrific story with you, my heart is heavy while Phoenix sits gazing at me as if nothing out of the ordinary had ever happened. That's my sweet, loving little man.

~Deborah Hodges

Additional Note: Phoenix was fortunate enough to receive medical care from the shelter through Susie's Miracle Fund.

 90

Susie's Special Friends
Bailey and Keely

Bailey was found on September 9, 2010, walking in a residential area of Greensboro, North Carolina. The people who found him took him to a local veterinarian's office and surrendered him as a "found dog."

The doctors immediately noticed that he was suffering from second- and third-degree burns down his entire back. He was then transported to the Guilford County Animal Shelter and named Bailey by one of the employees.

Bailey was fortunate enough to receive medical care from the shelter through Susie's Miracle Fund.

Around the time when Bailey was located, I read a news story about him on the Internet. The article showed a picture of Bailey and his horrific burns. I remember that he was looking directly at the camera with such a sad, pain-filled expression.

I had already been volunteering with the Susie's Law efforts and at events that raised money for Susie's Miracle Fund. I immediately felt a connection to Bailey and wanted to help him since, at the time, his case was unsolved.

In the mid-1990s, I volunteered with the McDowell County Humane Society. During that time I became a state-certified Animal Cruelty Investigator. I have always had a passion for all animals, especially the broken ones.

I was able to adopt Bailey and bring him home on October 14, 2010. I was told that he was around five years old. It was obvious from that first night that Bailey had been an indoor dog. He was so sweet and completely trusting. I began working on trying to find any information as to where he had come from and what had happened to him.

On April 9, 2011—while at an event benefiting Susie's Miracle Fund—I was told that Bailey's case had been officially closed by the police department. According to their investigation, the people who had originally found Bailey were the actual owners. They stated that Bailey was "accidentally" burned by their mentally handicapped son while he was giving Bailey a bath. The family kept Bailey at home for two days in an attempt to treat him. When they realized that his burns were too significant, they became scared and surrendered Bailey as a found animal. The case was deemed an accident, and no charges were ever pressed.

Bailey is scarred from the middle of his shoulder blades to the base of his tail. His hair will never grow back. He loves to sleep with me at night and begs to go for car rides.

Bailey now accompanies me to various Susie's Hope™ non-profit organization and Susie's Law events. He is very outgoing, and he loves treats and to be petted. I love to speak to citizens about cruelty to animals, the current laws regarding animals, and how to properly take care of a pet.

Due to Bailey's growing popularity, we created a Facebook page called "Bailey Greene" so that his story could be told.

Today Bailey is my best friend. He currently lives with a pit bull–golden retriever mix and a poodle mix. All three of them are rescued dogs. I believe that Bailey and I have a purpose together in life and we are lucky enough to be able to share our story.

~Keely Greene

The Susie's Hope™ Program Is...

The Susie's Hope™ program features a powerful message of love, hope, and forgiveness.

It's about:
- Facing your fears and watching them disappear.
- Getting a second chance at life and running with it.
- Never giving up hope.
- Loving and trusting again.
- Moving forward and not looking back.
- Living for the moment and not living in the past.
- Not holding on to the negative in life, but focusing on the positive.
- Forgiving those who hurt you and in that way, going from being a victim to being a victor.

Susie and I are on a personal journey to educate and inspire people about the importance of animal safety and animal care. We have been working together as a team to motivate people to love and respect their pets. Education is the best prevention when it comes to animal abuse.

We have been visiting schools, churches, organizations, our special-needs community, pet adoption fairs, and fundraisers. Soon we hope to visit hospitals and medical facilities to inspire burn victims and cancer patients, along with victims of any kind of violence and abuse.

We tell the story of two miracles—human and animal. Susie and I both survived a brutal attack and lived to tell about it.

Susie's Hope™ Pledge

I, _____, on this _____

day of _____ promise never to abuse,

neglect, torture, or bring harm in any way to any kind of animal.
I will love and respect all of God's creatures big and small.

To care for my pet, I will provide shelter, water, food, exercise,
groomings, and regular checkups. I promise to love and respect
my animal and to take care of my pet to the best of my ability.

Hand with paw, I will honor Susie's Law.

_____
Signature

Donna Lawrence

Donna's Signature

_____
Susie's Signature

In Susie's Words

One day a human hurt me really bad.
But to tell you what happened would make you sad.

Instead I will tell you a happy tale
Of all the loving people who made me well.

My friends at the shelter doctored me up
And made me once again a healthy pup.

As I got better, family and friends pitched in
To make sure I was healthy and happy again.

My forever mom, Donna, gave me a home
With unconditional love I had never known.

To keep my animal friends safe, no matter how small,
Hand with paw, Susie's Team and friends changed the law.

A happy ending is what we should share
With all of God's creatures, big and small, everywhere.

So love and respect your pets, and treat them right.
It's time to cuddle up with my mom and say goodnight.

~Susie

Susie's Trainer
Ally Thomas

Working with Donna and Susie has been my pleasure. Donna came to dog school with an open mind and a committed attitude. She wanted to learn how to manage Susie's behavior throughout the new public life that they were about to enter. They started like all of our students with obedience and learning theory. Once they mastered the basics, they moved on to canine acting so that they could entertain the public with tricks, fun skits, and skateboard riding.

I think they were both surprised how interesting and fun learning new things together can be and how much it enhances the bond between human and canine. Susie is one of the most amazing dogs that I have met in my 35-year career. When Susie is at school, she is "just one of the guys," but when it is time to go to work, she does a beautiful job of being the canine advocate for animal rights.

All of us at Southern Tails are so proud of her and Donna.

~Ally

Additional Notes

First Ally Thomas always says that we are the trainers and that she just assists and teaches us to teach our dogs. She has helped me teach Susie many tricks. Ally has assisted me to teach Susie all along the way.

Second you can read more about Susie's training by going to page 99 and reading the requirements for the American Kennel Club's Good Canine Citizen certification test. Susie has passed this and is certified. This allows her to go into schools and nursing homes.

~Donna

The American Kennel Club's (AKC)
Canine Good Citizen Certification Test

Demonstrating confidence and control, the dog must pass the following ten steps of the AKC Canine Good Citizen certification test:

1. Accepting a friendly stranger
2. Sitting politely for petting
3. Appearance and grooming
4. Walking on a loose lead/Out for a walk
5. Walking through a crowd
6. Staying in place/"Sit" and "down" on command
7. Coming when called
8. Meeting another dog
9. Reacting to distractions
10. Supervised separation
    The dog can be left with a trusted person, if necessary, and will retain training and good manners.

Susie's Tips for Taking Care of Your Dog

Pets are a great joy, but with that great joy comes great responsibility. Below are some basic tips for how to maintain and properly care for your dog.

1. Make sure that your dog has plenty of fresh, healthful food and water throughout the day. During the winter months, make sure the water isn't frozen. Try to avoid giving your dog table scraps.

2. Be sure to maintain proper shelter for an outside dog with a comfortable place to sleep and rest. A suitable doghouse should consist of at least three sides, a floor, and a roof. Durable fiber, wood, plastic, or other nonmetallic materials are the best materials to use for a doghouse. Avoid metal barrels; they do not provide protection from the heat and cold, and they do not enable an animal to maintain its adequate body temperature. Make sure the house is properly insulated; this can be done by using dry blankets, hay, or cedar chips. The shelter must be able to keep your dog dry and comfortable during all weather conditions such as rain, wind, sleet, and snow. The doghouse must be large enough to allow your pet

100

plenty of room to turn around, lie down, and stretch comfortably. During the summer months, the house should be placed in a shady area. During the winter months, the house should be placed away from the wind.

3. **Tips for a healthy pet:**

- Spay or neuter your pet. This will help your pet live a longer and healthier life. It also eliminates pet overpopulation.

- Make sure your pet gets plenty of exercise. Take him for a walk, using a leash, for at least 30 minutes a day. This will keep your pet in good health, both mentally and physically.

- Make sure your pet gets regular checkups by a veterinarian, including appropriate shots, heartworm medicine (once a month), and flea medication.

- Show your pet lots of love and affection, and provide playtime. This lets her know that she is a part of your family.

- Gently, firmly, and consistently discipline your pet. You must become the pack leader. Otherwise, your pet may become fearful and aggressive.

3. Tips for a healthy pet: (continued)

- Teach your dog basic commands such as sit, stay, down, heel, and come. This will exercise her brain as well as her body.

- Train instead of complain. Most pet problems can be solved with training, using treats, and using praise.

- Regular grooming is important. Keep nails trimmed, teeth cleaned, and hair brushed. Be sure that your pet gets bathed regularly using warm, soapy water.

- Make sure that your pet has a collar and a tag (with your address and phone number). This is for his safety, in case he gets lost.

- Keep pets inside your home if at all possible, or in a large, fenced-in yard. Pets that roam free face many dangers.

A righteous man cares for the needs of his animal.

Proverbs 12:10

Susie's Animal-Safety Tips

Millions of people are bitten by dogs each year. Some bites are minor; however, some can be very bad or even fatal.

1. **If you are playing outside and a dog is racing towards you, barking and baring its teeth, what should you do?**

   - Stand still—don't run or scream. Dogs chase moving objects, especially noisy ones.

   - Dogs tend to lose interest in someone who is standing still; they will usually sniff you, get bored, and walk away.

2. **Never approach a strange dog. When you approach a dog, be sure to do the following:**

   - Do not run up to the dog. This can make him feel threatened or scared, and in turn, he may attack you.

   - Do not make eye contact, and do not put your face at a dog's face level. You may get bitten on your face.

103

- Give the dog a treat, if you have one. You will earn her trust. Then proceed to approach the dog slowly.

3. **Before petting a dog, be sure to do the following:**
   - Always ask the pet's owner for permission to pet their dog. Also ask if the dog is friendly to strangers, or if there is a chance that their pet could bite you.

   - You may want to ask the dog's owner where her dog prefers to be petted.

   - Approach with caution. Pet the dog under her chin, on the side of her face, on the top of her head, or on her side.

   - Avoid petting a dog near his behind, since this may scare him; he cannot see what you are doing.

   - Use caution when petting an injured dog. Avoid petting her on her scars or injuries. This could hurt her or make her lash out at you.

4. Never do the following:

- Never reach around or attempt to hug a dog without the owner's permission.

- Never sneak up behind a dog and pull his tail. This could scare him and cause him to bite you.

- Never approach a dog that is fearful, angry, sleeping, or eating. Be careful around a dog that is eating; back away and never try to take her food, bone, or toy away from her.

- Never approach a dog that has been injured to try to help. Let the experts handle these situations—call animal control or the police.

- Never approach a dog that has just had puppies. They are very protective of their puppies.

- Never reach to pet dogs that are in cars, on chains, or behind fences.

- Never let your dog roam loose. Even the best dogs can bite strangers.

5. Helpful tips to remember:

- Be a good citizen to your dog.

- Dogs have feelings, just like humans. They can be happy, sad, afraid, angry, nervous, tired, or playful. Since dogs cannot talk, we must read their body language.

- Do not pet dogs when they are angry, afraid, sleeping, or protecting a person or an animal. Wait to pet them when they are happy and playful.

6. What to do if you are bitten by a dog:

- Tell an adult immediately so that your wounds can be cared for.

- The wound should be washed with warm, soapy water for ten minutes.

- As soon as you can, report the injury to your doctor, the police, and animal control. Tell them where and when you were bitten. Describe what the dog looked like, and tell them in which direction the dog was headed. This may prevent someone else from being bitten.

Closing Statement

In 2010, North Carolina citizens—with the help of State Representatives Maggie Jeffus and Pricey Harrison and State Senator Don Vaughan—passed the bill known as Susie's Law.

Susie's Law allows judges to give jail time to people convicted of animal abuse in North Carolina. We were all inspired by Susie, the poster dog for animal abuse and the sweet puppy that gave a voice to all abused animals in our state.

About the Author and Susie

Donna Lawrence is a native of Pine Hall, North Carolina. She was raised on a farm with her parents and seven brothers and sisters.

In October 2008, Donna was attacked by a pit bull and nearly died. Understandably, the attack left her extremely fearful of dogs, but that changed in August 2009. That is when she met Susie, the puppy that had been found beaten, burned, and left to die in a Greensboro, North Carolina, park. Susie has helped Donna overcome her fear of dogs and has given Donna new inspirations for life.

Donna is the Founder and Executive Director of the Susie's Hope™ nonprofit organization that educates children and adults about the importance of animal care and safety.

—⁓—

Susie resides with her mom and dad in High Point, North Carolina. Susie's tragic story became the motivation and inspiration behind Susie's Law that went into effect in North Carolina on December 1, 2010. Susie is a brindle pit bull/shepherd mix. She was adopted by Roy and Donna Lawrence from the Guilford County Animal Shelter on December 8, 2009. The Lawrences have helped Susie learn to love and respect humans who love and respect her.

About the Artist

Jennifer Tipton Cappoen has a bachelor's degree in fine arts from the University of North Carolina at Greensboro. She has spent more than 25 years honing her skills as an illustrator and a designer for both the educational and Christian publishing markets. Her work has been featured in publications by The Education Center, Inc.; New Day Publishing; True Hope Publishing Inc.; and Bayard Publishing. She lives in Greensboro, North Carolina, with her husband, Andrew, and their four dogs.